Women in Profile

Leaders in Medicine

Shaun Hunter

Crabtree Publishing Company

Dedication

This series is dedicated to every woman who has followed her dreams and to every young girl who hopes to do the same. While overcoming great odds and often oppression, the remarkable women in this series have triumphed in their fields. Their dedication, hard work, and excellence can serve as an inspiration to all—young and old, male and female. Women in Profile is both an acknowledgment of and a tribute to these great women.

Project Coordinator
Leslie Strudwick
Crabtree Editor
Virginia Mainprize
Editing and Proofreading
Carlotta Lemieux
Alana Luft
Krista McLuskey
Design
Warren Clark

Published by Crabtree Publishing Company

350 Fifth Avenue, Suite 3308
New York, NY
USA 10018

360 York Road, R.R. 4
Niagara-on-the-Lake
Ontario, Canada
L0S 1J0

Cataloging-in-Publication Data

Hunter, Shaun, 1961–
      Leaders in medicine / Shaun Hunter.
          p. cm — (Women in profile)
      Includes bibliographical references and index.
      Summary: Chronicles the lives and achievements of pioneering women in medicine, including cardiologist Helen Taussig, pathologist Alice Hamilton, psychoanalyst Anna Freud, and medical researcher Florence Sabin.
      ISBN 0-7787-0032-1 (pbk.) — ISBN 0-7787-0010-0 (rlb.)
      1. Women physicians—Biography—Juvenile literature.
2. Women medical scientists—Biography—Juvenile literature. 3. Women in medicine—History—20th century—Juvenile literature. [1. Women in medicine. 2. Physicians. 3. Women—Biography.] I. Title. II. Series.
R692.H86   1999
610'.92'2—ddc21
[B]
                              98-39281
                                    CIP
                                    AC

Photograph Credits
Every reasonable effort has been made to trace ownership and to obtain permission to reprint copyright material. The publishers would be pleased to have any errors or omissions brought to their attention so that they may be corrected in subsequent printings.

Archive Photos: pages 22, 24, 28, 42; Corbis-Bettmann: page 8; Image Works: page 44; Courtesy of Sylva Maubec: pages 30, 33, 34, 35; Moebes, Jack G./Corbis: page 18; Courtesy of NASA: page 43; National Library of Medicine: pages 6, 11, 13; Nienhuis Montessori: page 29; Radcliffe College Archives: cover, pages 36, 37, 38, 40, 41; Simon & Schuster: page 23; Dr. Anne Spoerry: pages 31, 32; Leslie Strudwick: page 7; University of Washington: page 10; University of Illinois at Chicago, Jane Addams Memorial Collection: pages 14, 15, 16, 17; UPI/Corbis-Bettmann: pages 12, 20, 21, 25, 26, 27, 39; Baldwin H. Ward/Corbis-Bettmann: page 9; Courtesy of Flossie Wong-Staal: page 45.

Contents

Leaders in Medicine

Throughout history, women have been leaders in medicine. In many ancient native cultures in Africa, North America, and Latin America, women healers played an important role. Long before 1 000 B.C., women surgeons practiced in China. There were women doctors in the Roman Empire. Through the ages, female nurses often carried out the same duties as **physicians**.

In modern times in the West, however, women came up against many barriers in the field of medicine. Until quite recently, most people considered a career in medicine unsuitable for a woman. Until the mid-1800s, medical schools shut their doors to women in North America and Europe. As a result, several North American women began to open their own medical schools and hospitals in the 1850s.

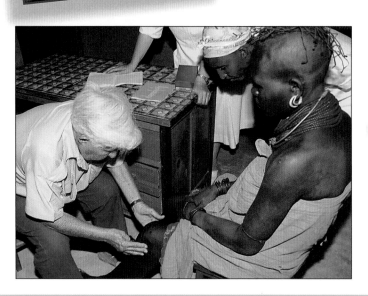

By the early 1900s, there were many women practicing medicine, but women doctors still had few opportunities. Hospitals limited the number of women who could gain practical experience by being **interns**. Gradually, attitudes changed, and more doors were opened for women in medicine. Today, up to half of all medical students are women, and many women are at the forefront of medical research.

Each of the women featured in this book has overcome obstacles to forge her career in medicine. These women are just a few of the many determined and committed female medical leaders in the twentieth century. The stories of their lives reveal how and why they chose medicine, and what they achieved. Each of the six major profiles examines the woman's early years, her training in medicine, and her accomplishments. The last section of the book provides brief descriptions of several other women medical leaders.

Perhaps the stories of these women and their lives will inspire you to follow your own dreams and make your contribution in the world of medicine.

Key Events

1920 Receives a medical degree from the University of Prague; marries fellow student Carl Cori

1922 Moves to Buffalo, New York, to do cancer research

1928 Becomes an American citizen

1931 Joins the University of Washington School of Medicine in St. Louis, Missouri, as a research associate

1936 Gives birth to a son, Carl Thomas

1947 Receives Nobel Prize in medicine and physiology; becomes ill with a rare form of fatal anemia

"For a research worker, the unforgotten moments of [one's] life are those rare ones, which come after years of plodding work, when the veil over nature's secret seems suddenly to lift."

Gerty Cori

Czechoslovakian Biochemist

Early Years

Gerty Radnitz grew up in Prague, the capital city of the country now known as the Czech Republic. A lively girl with a strong curiosity, she dreamed of being a scientist. Two people close to Gerty had scientific careers. Her father was a successful chemist in the sugar-refining business. Her uncle was a pediatrician—a children's doctor. Gerty's uncle encouraged her to go to medical school.

Medical schools in Prague accepted women, but most women had not studied the subjects required for acceptance. Gerty needed eight years of Latin, five years of math, and a solid foundation in chemistry and physics. The summer she turned sixteen, she and her family were on holiday in the Austrian Alps. There she met a teacher who offered to help her learn Latin.

By the end of the summer, Gerty had completed three years worth of Latin. She studied all the next year and was ready to take the entrance exam to medical school. She passed. Later in her life, Gerty called it "the hardest examination I was ever called upon to take."

Backgrounder

Prague

Prague is a beautiful, old European city with a rich history. At the turn of the century, Prague was home to people from many cultures, including Czechs, Germans, and Jews. The city had a long tradition as a center for artists, writers, and musicians. Its university attracted scholars from across Europe. When Gerty was growing up, Prague was part of the Austro-Hungarian Empire. During World War I, the empire collapsed and Prague became the capital of a new country, Czechoslovakia. In 1992, Czechoslovakia split into two countries: the Czech Republic and Slovakia. Prague became the capital city of the Czech Republic.

Prague is famous for its many beautiful, colorful buildings.

BACKGROUNDER

The Cori Partnership

Gerty and Carl's working partnership began in medical school when they wrote a scientific paper together. Later in their careers, it was hard for people to tell whether it was Gerty or Carl who had made a particular discovery, because they worked together so closely. They trusted each other's judgement and consulted each other frequently. Their personalities fitted together well too. Gerty was a keen researcher who loved the detective work of scientific discovery. Carl was more reserved and liked planning the overall direction of their work. In many ways, Gerty was leader of the team, but at first Carl got most of the credit. In the 1920s and 1930s, women scientists were paid less attention than men, and they were given smaller salaries.

Gerty and her husband made many significant discoveries as a team.

Developing Skills

At medical school in Prague, Gerty began to study biochemistry, a new and exciting field of science. Biochemistry deals with the chemical processes in living things—for example, what is happening inside cells. During her first year of studies, Gerty met Carl Cori, a shy medical student from Austria. They became friendly and worked on research projects together. In 1920, when Gerty finished medical school, she married Carl. Anxious to leave Europe, which was suffering from the effects of World War I, Gerty and Carl looked for jobs overseas.

In 1922, Carl moved to Buffalo, New York, to work at a well-known cancer research institute. Gerty joined him at the institute a few months later. She began to study how the body uses energy. She and Carl worked together closely on this project and published fifty scientific papers. Through Gerty's careful experiments with rats, the Coris observed

the way muscles use and store energy. At the time, scientists knew very little about this process. It is now known as the Cori Cycle and is studied as a basic part of high school science.

After spending nine years in Buffalo, the Coris decided to leave the cancer institute to continue their research in biochemistry. Many institutions offered Carl a position, but they did not offer Gerty one. At one interview, Gerty was told it was "un-American" for a wife to work with her husband.

The Coris finally accepted positions at the University of Washington in St. Louis, Missouri. Carl became a full professor and head of a department. Gerty was employed as a research associate with a much lower salary than Carl's. Although she and Carl had equal qualifications, she had to wait thirteen years before she became a full professor.

"I believe that the benefits of two civilizations, a European education followed by the freedom and opportunities of [the United States], have been essential to whatever contributions I have been able to make in science."

Even though she had as much experience as her husband, Gerty did not receive as much recognition for her work.

Quick Notes

- Gerty loved the outdoors. She and Carl used to hike, ski, and climb in the Rockies and the Alps.

- In Buffalo, Gerty studied the effects of x-rays on the body. This work may have brought about her illness later in life.

- Gerty and Carl traveled throughout the world to find treatment for Gerty's illness.

- President Truman appointed Gerty to the National Science Foundation. She attended meetings in spite of her illness. Before each flight to Washington, D.C., she received a blood transfusion.

Accomplishments

At the University of Washington, Gerty's work took a new direction. She and Carl had begun studying enzymes, the **proteins** that control most of the chemical reactions in the body. The laboratory buzzed with Gerty's excitement for her research. One of her fellow workers remembers Gerty jumping up and down after a particular success. Whenever Gerty had important news, she ran down the hall to share it with Carl. Their research attracted a lot of attention, and scientists from across the world came to study with them. Eight future Nobel Prize winners worked or trained in Gerty's lab.

Gerty demanded perfection from her staff and trained them carefully. She knew that the tiniest impurity would destroy her experiments. Her laboratory was a challenging place to work. Every day, the staff gathered over sandwich lunches for scientific discussions with Gerty and Carl. On Friday afternoons, they discussed the latest scientific articles. Gerty herself read five to seven books a week on a variety of topics. She arranged for the library staff to send her new scientific journals before they were placed on the shelves.

The University of Washington.

Through their research, Gerty and Carl identified the enzymes that change the sugar used by muscle cells for energy into its stored form. In 1947, they were awarded the Nobel Prize for this work. The Nobel committee called their discovery "one of the most brilliant achievements in modern history."

In the summer of 1947, just before she learned about the Nobel Prize, Gerty fell ill. On a mountain-climbing trip in the Colorado Rockies, she collapsed. She had a rare blood disease.

Gerty continued her research for ten more years, though this was more and more difficult. As she grew weaker, she rested on a cot in the laboratory. A month before she died, Carl carried her from room to room at the laboratory. In spite of her illness, Gerty completed some of her most important work during the final years of her life.

BACKGROUNDER
The Nobel Prize

The Nobel Prize in medicine and **physiology** is one of the most highly respected prizes in science. The Coris were awarded the prize for studies on how muscles in the body use sugar. Gerty was the first woman to receive the Nobel Prize in medicine and physiology. The day she and Carl learned of their Nobel Prize, they went to work as usual. When they were in Stockholm to accept the prize, they each delivered a part of their Nobel lecture. Back home, they shared their $24,460 in prize money with several scientists working in their laboratory.

"The love for and dedication to one's work seems to me to be the basis for happiness."

Gerty's love for research gave her the strength to continue working in spite of serious illness.

KEY EVENTS

1893 Graduates with a medical degree from University of Michigan

1897 Moves to Hull House, a community shelter in Chicago

1910 Heads Occupational Disease Commission for State of Illinois

1919 Becomes the first woman to serve on the faculty of Harvard University Medical School

1924–30 Serves on a health committee at the League of Nations in Geneva

1925 Publishes the book *Industrial Poisoning in the United States*

1935 Becomes professor emeritus of industrial medicine at Harvard University

"*I chose [medicine] because as a doctor I could go anywhere I pleased—to far-off lands or to city slums—and could be quite sure that I could be of use anywhere.*"

Alice Hamilton

American Pathologist

Early Years

A lice was born in New York City but spent her childhood in Fort Wayne, Indiana. Her family lived on a big estate that had been built by Alice's grandfather, a successful businessman. Alice grew up surrounded by her cousins, aunts, and uncles, as well as her sisters. Her father did not like public schools, so he hired private teachers to instruct his children at home. As Alice later remarked, "We learned what our parents thought important: languages, literature, history." Alice and her sisters were also taught to think for themselves.

Alice's mother wanted her daughters to be well educated and have careers. This was an unusual attitude in the United States in the late 1800s. When Alice was seventeen, she was sent to a girls school in Connecticut for two years. While she was there, her father's wholesale grocery business failed. Alice realized she would have to support herself. Since she wanted to make a difference in people's lives, she decided to become a doctor.

BACKGROUNDER

The Hamilton Sisters

Alice had three sisters. She also had one brother, but he was not born until she was seventeen. Alice was particularly close to her sister Edith, who was three years older. As a child, Edith had a passion for classic Greek literature. Like Alice, she was encouraged by her parents to pursue her own interests. She became a noted Greek scholar and wrote several books about Greek classics.

Alice knew that she would have to work very hard to succeed in medicine.

Developing Skills

Alice's education had not prepared her well for medical studies. She had little background in math or science, but she was determined to become a doctor. When she returned to Fort Wayne, she hired a local schoolteacher to tutor her in chemistry and physics. She enrolled in an **anatomy** course at the local medical school. Four years later, Alice was accepted at the University of Michigan's medical school. One year later, at the age of twenty-four, she graduated with a medical degree.

Alice wanted to continue her medical career in research. She was particularly interested in the field of pathology, the study of diseased body organs and cells. One of her professors convinced her to get some hospital experience first by working as an **intern**. At the time, most hospitals would not accept women as interns, but Alice found a position at the New England Hospital for Women and Children in Boston. Most of the patients in this hospital were desperately poor. For the first time, Alice realized how much poor people suffered.

Alice's hard work and determination paid off. She became a successful doctor and researcher.

"Though I did not feel competent to treat sick babies, I did venture to open a well-baby clinic."

After her internship, Alice went to study in Germany, where ground-breaking work in pathology was being carried out. When she returned to the United States, she continued her studies at Johns Hopkins Medical School in Baltimore. She began her first job in Chicago as a professor of pathology at the Women's Medical College at Northwestern University.

Alongside her teaching duties at the medical college, Alice did volunteer work at a community center called Hull House. The center was in one of the poorest neighborhoods of Chicago's West Side and was used mostly by immigrants. Here Alice found her true calling. She set up a baby clinic in the basement and taught mothers the importance of keeping their babies clean. At the time, there were no baby clinics in Chicago.

In 1902, a typhoid **epidemic** broke out in Chicago. Alice proved that flies were spreading typhoid germs. As a result of her findings, changes were made to the city's health department, and the city's drinking water was made safer.

BACKGROUNDER
Hull House

In 1889, the social reformer Jane Addams opened the doors of an old building in the slums of Chicago. Hull House was a settlement house, or community center. Volunteers lived at Hull House and provided their services to help the poor. Neighborhood children could stay at the day nursery or attend kindergarten while their parents worked. A public kitchen served meals to people in need. A playground and social rooms were provided for recreation. When Alice returned from her studies in Europe, she heard Jane Addams speak in Fort Wayne. She was so impressed that she decided to work with her.

At Hull House, Alice was able to provide care and education for the poor.

Backgrounder

Lead Poisoning

The thing Alice most wanted to find during her survey of Illinois factories was the cause of lead poisoning. People with lead poisoning suffer from headaches, weakness, and violent shaking, among other things. Sometimes they die. In Alice's day, people thought lead poisoning was caused by having dirty hands. Alice visited factories that used lead and interviewed officials. She examined the medical records of poisoned workers and talked with their families. She finally decided that workers were being poisoned by breathing lead fumes and dust. As a result of her study, factory owners gradually improved conditions for people working with lead.

Accomplishments

At Hull House, Alice carefully observed the lives of the families she served. She noticed that men working in factories and steel mills became sick and sometimes died. At the time, the health and safety of workers was not a major concern in the United States. Sickness and death were seen as normal risks in the life of a laborer. Workers had no legal protection against unsafe workplaces.

Alice began talking and writing about health problems among workers and about dangerous workplaces. She told people about her findings on a disease called "phossy jaw" that affected people working at match factories in Chicago. Workers were breathing in **phosphorus** fumes that killed the roots of their teeth and damaged their jawbones. After Alice drew attention to the problem, the match factories replaced phosphorus with a harmless substance.

Alice had so much to say about public health in Chicago that the governor of Illinois made her director of the state's survey of poison in industry. This survey was the first of its kind in the United States. Alice and a team of twenty doctors, medical students, and social workers inspected factories and examined dozens of people who had become sick working there. Alice's recommendations resulted in new laws in Illinois to protect workers. These laws became models for other states.

Alice worked with a team to make conditions better for workers.

In 1919, Alice left Chicago and Hull House to become the first woman professor at Harvard Medical School. Alice continued to examine unsafe substances and workplaces throughout the country. She also traveled to Europe and the Soviet Union to study health and safety there.

Alice often took a stand on things that were unpopular in her day. At a time when talking about **birth control** was simply not done, Alice supported women's right to decide whether or not to have children. Before World War I, she joined a group that wanted peace. After World War II, she encouraged the United States government to recognize the **communist** People's Republic of China. Throughout her long life, as a **physician**, reformer, and educator, Alice remained true to herself and her beliefs.

"I looked with a little envy at the women doctors [in the Soviet Union], for never before had I been in a country where men and women in medicine are absolutely equal."

Although being a woman physician presented many challenges, Alice persevered and enjoyed a long and successful career.

Quick Notes

- In 1943, Alice published a book about her life called *Exploring the Dangerous Trades.*

- In 1995, the United States Post Office issued the Alice Hamilton fifty-five cent stamp as part of its Great Americans series.

- After Alice moved to Boston to teach at Harvard University in 1919, she continued to volunteer at Hull House in Chicago several weeks each year until 1935.

- When Alice joined Harvard Medical School, there were no other women on staff and no women medical students. Alice was not allowed to use the all-male Harvard Club, nor could she take part in graduation ceremonies. During her fifteen-year career at Harvard, she was never promoted from her position as assistant professor.

"I learn always from dying patients. Instead of always looking at the negative, what you see is the uniqueness and strength in every single human being."

Elisabeth Kübler-Ross

Swiss Psychiatrist

Early Years

Elisabeth Kübler started her life fighting. She was the first-born of triplets—three little girls. Doctors did not expect the tiny baby to survive. Elisabeth defied the odds and grew into a strong-willed, independent girl. From an early age, she felt different from her sisters. She wanted to be recognized on her own merits, not treated as part of a threesome.

As a child, Elisabeth had a passion for science. She set up a small laboratory in her family's basement in her hometown outside Zurich, Switzerland. There she conducted experiments and started an animal "hospital." In sixth grade, she wrote an essay about her dreams for the future. She wanted to be "a researcher and explorer of unknown frontiers of knowledge." Above all, she wanted to be a **physician**.

BACKGROUNDER

Switzerland during World War II

Switzerland is a small European country surrounded by France, Germany, Austria, and Italy. During World War II, Switzerland remained a neutral territory. It did not take an active part in the war but protected its borders with a well-trained army. Over the course of the war, thousands of refugees from surrounding countries sought safety in Switzerland. Many were Jews fleeing from the Nazis.

BACKGROUNDER

International Voluntary Service for Peace

IVSP was formed after World War I. It recruited people from different countries, backgrounds, and experiences to help communities in need throughout the world. None of the volunteers was paid for working with the service. The IVSP was one of the models for the American Peace Corps formed by President Kennedy in 1961. CUSO, the Canadian volunteer organization, was also based partly on IVSP.

Developing Skills

E lisabeth's father wanted her to join him in the office supply business, but Elisabeth was determined to become a researcher and doctor. At the age of sixteen, against her father's will, she set out on her own. For the following three years, she was an **apprentice** at a Zurich eye clinic, training to be a laboratory technician. This training prepared her to enter medical school.

During her years as an apprentice, Elisabeth did unpaid work with the International Voluntary Service for Peace. This group helped communities rebuild after World War II. Instead of taking vacation time from her job at the eye clinic, Elisabeth traveled throughout Europe working as a cook and laborer. She saw first-hand the effect of the war on people's lives. This experience increased Elisabeth's desire to become a physician.

At the eye clinic, Elisabeth grew less and less interested in the work she was doing in the laboratory. She preferred working directly with patients. She believed patients needed to have someone to listen to them and sympathize with their problems. Elisabeth learned to listen carefully and answer questions directly.

Elisabeth believed in the importance of listening to patients.

In Switzerland in the 1950s, medical school consisted of eight years of course work and exams. Most of Elisabeth's girlfriends were choosing to marry and have families, but Elisabeth had a different goal. She enrolled in medical school. She spent her days in class and studied during the evenings and on weekends. She paid her fees by working part-time in the eye clinic. In Elisabeth's medical courses, she often saw patients being treated more like laboratory specimens than human beings. She thought this very heartless. Some of the patients could not be cured and were dying of their illness.

For a woman in her twenties, Elisabeth had a great deal of experience with death. As a peace service volunteer, she had helped people who were grieving over the death of their loved ones. On a stay in Poland, she saw the Nazi **concentration camps**, where Jewish people had been imprisoned and killed during the war. She had personal experience with death, too. Her beloved brother-in-law died of cancer.

"The fear of death is the most inescapable fear of human beings and the most unavoidable one."

Elisabeth wrote a number of books to help people understand and cope with death.

Quick Notes

- Elisabeth founded the American Holistic Medicine Association.

- Students at the University of Chicago named Elisabeth "most popular teacher" five years in a row.

- In 1979, the *Ladies' Home Journal* named Elisabeth one of the ten Women of the Decade.

- Elisabeth had a particular interest in helping dying children. In 1983, she published *On Children and Dying*.

Accomplishments

A t medical school, Elisabeth fell in love with an American medical student, Emmanuel Ross. She married him and moved with him to New York City, where she trained as a **psychiatrist**.

In the early 1960s, Emmanuel and Elisabeth moved to Denver, Colorado, where Elisabeth taught at the medical school. For her first lecture, she chose the topic of death and dying. She believed that medical students and doctors did not talk enough about death. Elisabeth wanted to show that dying patients had special needs. She asked a sixteen-year-old girl dying of **leukemia** to answer questions from the audience. Students attending the lecture were shocked by Elisabeth's direct handling of the subject.

Elisabeth believes in life after death.

"I work with dying children and they always draw butterflies. Dying is nothing else but a butterfly coming out of a cocoon."

Elisabeth continued to deal with death and dying after she moved to the University of Chicago in 1965. Several students training to be ministers and priests asked her to give workshops. They felt ill-prepared to counsel dying people. The weekly workshops were soon crowded with ministers, nurses, and social workers. As before, Elisabeth invited dying patients to answer questions at each session, though her fellow doctors objected strongly. They said she was taking advantage of people who were weak and helpless. Elisabeth replied that these patients were eager to share their feelings.

Over time, Elisabeth began to reach a wider audience with her lectures. She was asked to put her ideas into a book. When *On Death and Dying* was published in 1969, it became one of the most popular non-fiction books ever printed. Meanwhile, the doctors at the University of Chicago Medical School still objected to Elisabeth's style and message. They forbade her to use patients in her workshops, and they ended the lectures.

Elisabeth resigned and set out on her own. She had no difficulty spreading her message. People across the world invited her to speak to them. Elisabeth also helped introduce the hospice movement in North America to provide specialized care for dying patients. Her ground-breaking work has helped doctors and nurses all over the world understand the special needs of the dying.

BACKGROUNDER
On Death and Dying

Elisabeth took only three months to write her popular book *On Death and Dying*. The book represents Elisabeth's many years of work with hundreds of people dying from various illnesses. From her conversations with them, Elisabeth found there are usually five phases in a patient's reaction to death. First comes denial, then anger, bargaining with God to delay death, then depression, and finally acceptance. Health-care workers have since used these five stages to help people suffering from mental problems. For several years after *On Death and Dying* was published, Elisabeth received three thousand letters each month from people who had read her book or been to one of her workshops.

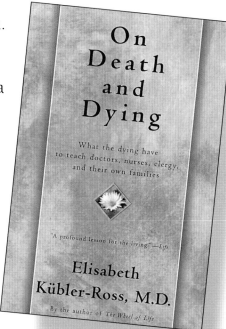

On
Death
and
Dying

What the dying have to teach doctors, nurses, clergy, and their own families

"A profound lesson for the living."—*Life*

Elisabeth
Kübler-Ross, M.D.

By the author of *The Wheel of Life*

First published in 1969, On Death and Dying *is still being sold around the world.*

"The nature of education should follow from an understanding of the child."

Maria Montessori

Italian Physician and Educator

Early Years

M aria was born in a small Italian town on the Adriatic Sea. Later, her family moved to Rome, where Maria enrolled at a technical school. She was twelve years old at the time. Most of her girlfriends left school at that age, but Maria was a keen student with a passion for math. She wanted to continue her studies.

By the time Maria graduated from technical school, she had decided to become a **physician**. Her friends and relatives were shocked. Medicine was not considered a suitable career for a woman. In Italy, women were not even permitted to attend medical school. Maria refused to be discouraged. She enrolled at the University of Rome to study math and science as an undergraduate. Two years later, she was admitted to medical school. Maria had persuaded the authorities to relax the rules in her case.

BACKGROUNDER

Maria's Family

Maria's father strongly disapproved of her plan to become a doctor. For many years, he distanced himself from her because of what he called her "rebellious nature." On the other hand, Maria's mother was very encouraging. Unlike most Italian women of her generation, Maria's mother was well educated. She was interested in the many changes occurring in Italian society at the time. She believed deeply in her daughter's talents and urged Maria to reach as high as she could.

Maria was very interested in engineering before she decided to study medicine.

Developing Skills

Many obstacles stood in Maria's way as the only woman at medical school. Because women were not allowed to walk in the streets alone, someone had to accompany her to class each day. The medical school had to make special arrangements for Maria to study human **anatomy** by herself in the evenings. It was considered improper for a woman to study the human body alongside men. At lectures, Maria had to wait until all the male students were seated before she could sit down. Her fellow students often made life difficult for her, but she ignored their nasty comments and calmly went about her studies.

Gradually, the students and professors noticed that Maria's work was of a very high quality. In her fourth year of medical school, Maria won an important scholarship. By then, the same students who had bullied her had come to admire this intelligent and charming young woman.

Maria's professors at medical school respected her interest and hard work.

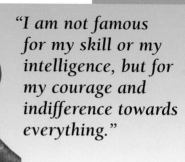

"I am not famous for my skill or my intelligence, but for my courage and indifference towards everything."

During her first years as a practicing doctor, Maria studied children who were mentally handicapped. She believed that these children did not have to be lost souls but could learn if given special help. This was not a popular view at the time.

Maria decided to use her medical knowledge in an educational setting. She helped set up a special school for mentally disadvantaged children. There, teams of doctors and teachers explored ways to educate them. Maria began to develop a set of teaching materials and methods so that the children could learn through their senses. After only three months, the children at the school were beginning to learn. Their progress was considered remarkable.

BACKGROUNDER

Helping Children with Disabilities

In the 1890s in Italy, there was little hope for children who had mental disabilities. They were placed in prison-like hospitals or left alone to wander the streets. During her frequent visits to a mental hospital in Rome, Maria watched children pick up bread crumbs—not to eat, but to play with. She realized that these children were able to learn and ought to be in school. She believed that by educating disadvantaged children, society as a whole would improve.

Maria was the first person in Italy to recognize the social benefits of educating disadvantaged children.

BACKGROUNDER

The Children's House

The young children at the first Casa dei Bambini were a human laboratory for Maria. She watched the way they used the activities she had designed. She saw their confidence and understanding grow each day. She gave them everyday chores, such as gardening and tidying up, and supplied child-sized furniture for the classroom. Maria asked the teacher to act as an observer and let the children choose their own activities. By watching the children teach themselves, Maria created her theory of education.

Accomplishments

Maria stayed with the school for mentally handicapped children for two years. She eventually returned to university to study the way children learn. During her studies, she decided that Italy's schools needed to change. She became convinced that most children would benefit from the same methods she had used with handicapped children. In 1906, a businessman approached Maria with an idea. He wanted her to start a center for young children in one of his low-income housing projects in Rome. His aim was to raise the value of his property by keeping children from running wild, but Maria had a different aim. She saw this as an opportunity to put her ideas about education to work in a real situation. She accepted the challenge, and in 1907 the Casa dei Bambini (Children's House) was born.

At the Casa dei Bambini, Maria was able to use her ideas about teaching children.

The success of the Children's House quickly attracted public attention. Soon, similar programs were begun in the Italian city of Milan and in Switzerland. In 1909, Maria published a book that explained her ideas and her special methods of teaching. *The Montessori Method* spread her ideas to educators throughout the world. Only two years later, public schools in Italy and Switzerland adopted her system.

With the success of her book, Maria closed her medical practice and worked full-time as an educator. She traveled and lectured throughout Europe and the United States, and later went to India. Her method became a profitable business. She supervised all teacher training at her home in Rome. She was completely committed to the success of her method and kept full control of it. She did not permit any changes.

Maria's ideas have greatly influenced the way schools are run today. Most modern schools do not look like those Maria attended as a child. They are no longer rigid places where students have to memorize information that is passed on from a teacher or a textbook. As a doctor and educator, Maria was amazed by the ability of all young children to learn. In them, she saw hope for a better future.

Maria's methods of teaching have had a great influence on education. There are now many Montessori schools throughout the world.

Quick Notes

- **Maria was an inspiring public speaker. Elegant and attractive, she always captured the attention of the media. In all of her many speeches and lectures, she never used notes. The papers she occasionally brought to the platform were just blank sheets she used as props.**

- **Early in her career, Maria spoke out in favor of women's rights. In 1896, at age twenty-six, she attended an international women's conference in Berlin, Germany, as a representative of Italy. She asked the members of the conference to support a proposal to try and get women paid the same as men for work of equal value.**

- **In her later years, Maria traveled widely. She saw herself as a citizen of the world and asked that she be buried wherever she died. She passed away in the Netherlands at the age of eighty-two.**

"I have seen Africa at its best and worst. I have known it in joy and sorrow.... I believe that the best is yet to come, and that come it will."

Anne Spoerry

French Physician

Early Years

As a young girl, Anne was eager for adventure. She describes herself as "something of a tomboy" who shared a love of sailing with her brother and father. When she was twelve, her parents sent her to boarding school in England for two years. Never homesick, Anne had a marvelous time. As a teenager, she often traveled with her family. These family trips gave Anne a lasting love of travel.

Anne grew up in the Alsace region of France, which had once been part of Germany. She could speak French, German, and English. By the time Anne had finished high school, she had decided to study medicine. Even as a child, she had wanted to become a doctor. Her favorite game had been operating on her rag doll and sewing it up again.

In 1937, Anne moved to Paris to study sciences. When World War II started in 1939, she was doing her medical training at the Saltpêtrière Hospital in Paris. By the spring of 1940, France had surrendered to the Germans, and much of France, including Paris, was controlled by the German army.

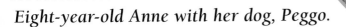

Eight-year-old Anne with her dog, Peggo.

BACKGROUNDER

Living in Occupied France

Anne remembers living in "occupied" France, where the Germans were in control. Although she had permission to move about freely as a medical student, she was often stopped and questioned by police. Anne joined her brother in his work with the French Resistance movement. She ran a house in Paris where Allied soldiers were hidden from German soldiers. Anne's brother was arrested in 1943. A few days later, Anne was arrested and sent to a **concentration camp**. She was released two years later at the end of the war. Anne's vivid memories of her travels helped keep her spirits up during this difficult time.

Developing Skills

After the war, Anne continued her medical studies. When she finished, she planned to leave war-torn Europe and start a new life in another part of the world. In 1948, Anne set sail for Aden, a city on the coast of Arabia. She served as the ship's doctor to Muslim pilgrims traveling to the holy city of Mecca in Saudi Arabia. She also worked in the women's ward of a hospital for Arab patients.

"It is extremely rewarding to work in these conditions where you really make a difference to life and death situations."

In 1949, Anne traveled to Kenya to visit friends. Moved by the beauty of the country, she decided to stay. Because she was a woman, she had difficulty getting work as a doctor. An unmarried woman was not considered a suitable person to be a doctor in the African countryside.

Anne finally found a job as a country doctor in a farming community. She was the only doctor looking after sixty farms. Each farm housed about two hundred people—the farming family and their workers. There were no telephones, and messengers brought Anne the news that someone was sick. She often visited her patients on horseback.

Riding horses was the only way to get to patients in the African countryside.

The 1950s were unstable years in Kenya. There was fighting between the native Kikuyu people and the British who ruled the **colony**. Anne provided first aid to the wounded. She visited her patients at night when it was safer to travel, and she always had dogs for protection.

After Kenya became independent in 1963, Europeans were forced to sell their land so that Africans could have their own farms. This was a depressing time for Anne. Like her fellow Europeans, she had been uprooted from her adopted home. She sold the large farm she had bought a few years earlier. Anne was not ready to leave Kenya, but she felt uncertain about her future. Looking for a new direction, she started to take flying lessons. She was forty-five years old.

BACKGROUNDER

Kenya's Independence

In the early 1900s, Kenya was under British rule. Europeans were settling the vast farmlands of Kenya. Often, their farms displaced African tribes. By the 1920s, Africans began to speak out against the British government. They felt they were not being treated fairly. In the 1950s, a secret organization of Africans, the Mau Mau, carried out armed attacks on European farmers, and many lives were lost. After the rebellion, the British introduced reforms. In 1963, Kenya became an independent nation.

Anne learned to fly a plane so she could continue to bring medical care to those in need.

BACKGROUNDER

African Medical and Research Foundation (AMREF)

AMREF was started by three doctors working in Kenya in the 1950s. They saw that people living in remote regions of East Africa had no medical services. The doctors set up a small network of two physicians, a handful of planes, and a radio system. In this way, they were able to send medical staff in and carry patients out for additional care. This program came to be known as the Flying Doctors of East Africa. The AMREF also established health centers in communities that had no access to medical services. These health centers trained local staff in the methods of preventing illness. Today, AMREF has a staff of nearly 650, almost all African.

Accomplishments

Anne quickly became a keen pilot. She bought a small farm as close to an airfield as possible. In 1964, she purchased her own plane. Soon afterwards, she became one of two flying doctors in the African Medical and Research Foundation.

As a flying doctor, Anne provided medical services to Africans living in remote areas. She relied on radio to learn who needed her help. With her plane and radio, Anne said she was "always completely mobile and ready for instant action." She also built a small clinic next to her house so that she could see local people there.

As a French doctor in Africa, Anne had to learn how to communicate easily with her patients. Over the years she learned how to speak Swahili, a language understood by most of the thirty-eight different ethnic groups in Kenya. She also had to learn about the culture and beliefs of her patients and their suspicion of modern medicine. As a new doctor in the Kenyan bush, she was at first intolerant of patients who were also seeing African medicine men. Gradually, Anne realized that seeing a medicine man often helped a patient's treatment. "The two work together," she said.

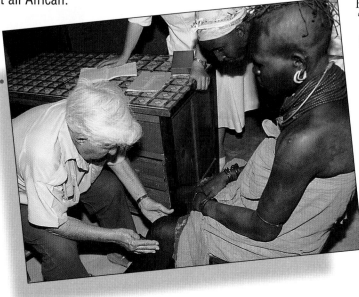

Learning their culture and language helped Anne in her work with African patients.

As well as treating their ailments, Anne did much to educate her patients. She stressed the importance of cleanliness as a way of avoiding illness. She persuaded parents to get their children immunized against **polio**, **smallpox**, and other serious diseases. She also taught women methods of **birth control** so that they could limit the size of their families. Kenyans tended to have very big families, with six or more children to feed and clothe.

Now in her eighties, Anne has officially retired as a flying doctor. She still flies to Kenyan outposts in her Piper Cherokee airplane filled with medical supplies and fresh vegetables from her garden. As a volunteer, she continues to set out on what she calls her "medical safaris," where she is cheerfully welcomed as "Mama Daktari," Swahili for Madam Doctor.

"I get much amusement from telling people that I am a doctor, electrician, postman and breakdown-mechanic all rolled into one."

Dr. Spoerry considers Africa her home, and is still active in medicine.

Quick Notes

- In 1996, Anne published a book about her life, *They Call Me Mama Daktari*.

- During her first years in Kenya, Anne founded a girl guide troop, the first in her area of Ol Kalou. She organized camps on her farm and gave young people a way of escaping the violence that was spreading across the country.

- Anne has noticed the changes in African women during her years in Kenya. Traditionally, women of the Kikuyu tribe were owned by their husbands. Today, many Kikuyu women are taking control of their own lives.

- In 1965, one year after she received her pilot's license, Anne flew to Europe for her summer holidays in her own single-engine plane. Her friends thought she was crazy. Anne wondered if they would have reacted this way if she were a man.

"Basically I am a scientist. A good research doctor has curiosity, persistence and a willingness to work hard."

Helen Taussig

American Pediatric Cardiologist

Early Years

Helen grew up in a family of scholars. Her mother was one of the first women to graduate from Radcliffe College, a women's college associated with Harvard University. Helen's father was a professor at Harvard. At high school, Helen was one of the top students in her class, but she had worked hard to achieve this. Early in her schooling, she had great difficulty reading. At the time, no one knew she had a learning disability called dyslexia.

During her childhood, Helen became sick with whooping cough which damaged her hearing. When Helen was eleven, her mother died of tuberculosis. With the support of her father, Helen found ways to cope with her problems. An excellent student, she was accepted by Radcliffe College in her hometown of Cambridge, Massachusetts. She later transferred to the University of California at Berkeley on the other side of the country. By the time she graduated, she had decided on a career in medicine.

BACKGROUNDER

Dyslexia

Dyslexia is a learning disability. People with dyslexia have trouble reading and spelling. Letters or words often appear reversed. Although they are intelligent, many dyslexic people do not learn to read or write easily. Until recently, learning disabilities such as dyslexia were not widely recognized. Now dyslexic children have much greater support.

Radcliffe College opened in 1879.

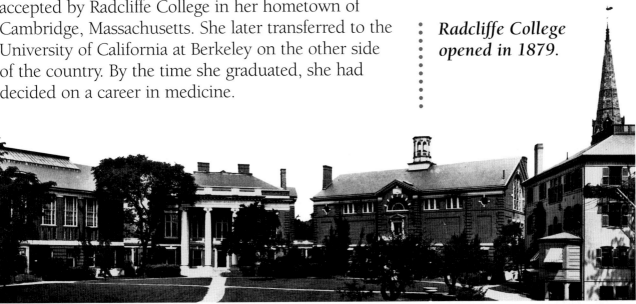

Developing Skills

H elen's route to medical school was not direct. In the 1920s, very few medical schools in the United States accepted women. Only six percent of American **physicians** were women. Helen's father encouraged her to apply to a new school of public health. Helen soon learned that although women could attend classes, they would not be granted degrees.

Helen was determined to become a doctor. She enrolled in an **anatomy** class at Boston University. One day, her professor handed her an ox heart to study. Helen **dissected** the heart and carried out successful experiments with the heart muscle that had not been done before. Impressed by her work, the professor suggested she apply to Johns Hopkins Medical School in Baltimore, Maryland. Johns Hopkins was one of the best medical schools in the country and one of the few to admit women.

Four years later, Helen received her medical degree. She applied to be an **intern** in internal medicine at Johns Hopkins Hospital. The hospital only allowed one woman intern in that field, and they already had one. Helen decided to specialize in pediatrics, which turned out to be very lucky for her and for thousands of children around the world. In 1930, Helen joined a new department at the hospital that focused on heart problems in children. **Pediatric cardiology** was a brand new field of medicine, and Helen was to become one of its pioneers.

> *"I didn't know it but others had tried similar experiments with heart and muscle and failed. Having no idea it couldn't be done, I just tried and it worked. I was not hampered by being told it was impossible."*

When Helen graduated from medical school, there were few women physicians in the United States.

At the clinic, Helen used new types of equipment to examine children's hearts. She was able to observe how the heart worked while it was beating. The children Helen saw at the clinic were believed to be untreatable. Many were very small for their age and breathed with great difficulty. Their skin, lips, and fingertips looked blue because of lack of oxygen. Doctors call this condition "cyanosis," from the Greek word for blue, *cyan*.

Helen spent a great deal of time thinking about cyanotic children, or "blue babies." For fourteen years, she studied the problem. She examined hundreds of patients but did not know how to help them. Eventually, she came up with the idea of operating on them. Helen asked the surgeon Alfred Blalock to help her, and he agreed. For three years, Dr. Blalock worked in the laboratory, testing the operation on dogs. At the time, surgery to repair the human heart was rarely if ever carried out.

Backgrounder
Blue Babies

When Helen started her medical career, there was no cure for cyanotic children—"blue babies." Doctors thought these children died of heart failure. After many years of studying them, Helen believed that cyanotic children died because their blood was not getting enough oxygen from the lungs. She knew that these children would get more oxygen if more blood could flow to the lungs. With the surgeon Alfred Blalock, Helen developed an artificial **artery** to bypass the blocked blood vessel connecting the heart to the lungs. This new artery became known as the Blalock-Taussig shunt. It paved the way for developments in open-heart surgery. Today, cyanotic children receive open-heart surgery to repair their condition.

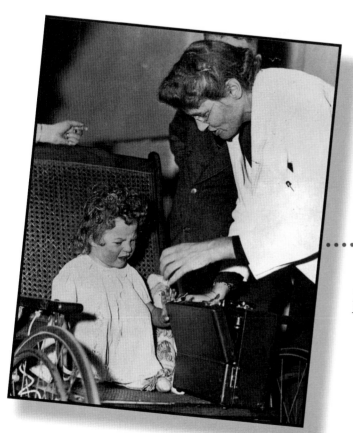

Many cyanotic children were saved by the heart operation Helen developed.

Quick Notes

- At university, Helen was a champion tennis player.

- Helen published more than a hundred scientific articles during her career, forty of them after she retired from Johns Hopkins Hospital.

- In her eighties, Helen began a study of bird hearts to try and find the causes of certain heart defects.

- Heart doctors considered Helen's book on heart problems to be very important. One doctor remembers holding a stethoscope in one hand and Helen's book in the other while consulting with patients.

- Helen spent most of her working life with impaired hearing. To communicate with her patients, she learned to read lips, wore a hearing aid, and asked patients to write down their thoughts. After she retired, an operation restored her hearing.

Helen's gentle nature put her patients at ease.

Accomplishments

By 1944, Helen's team was ready to operate on a cyanotic child. The fourteen-month-old baby girl was very underweight and had been living in an oxygen tent for three months. After the operation, the baby gradually improved, and she lived for another six months. Although the baby died, Helen did not consider the operation a failure, because the child's condition did get better for awhile.

From then on, each operation the team carried out was more successful. News of the wonderful results of the Blalock-Taussig shunt spread quickly. Soon, Helen was seeing patients from across North America and around the world. In the first five years, more than one thousand cyanotic children were operated on successfully.

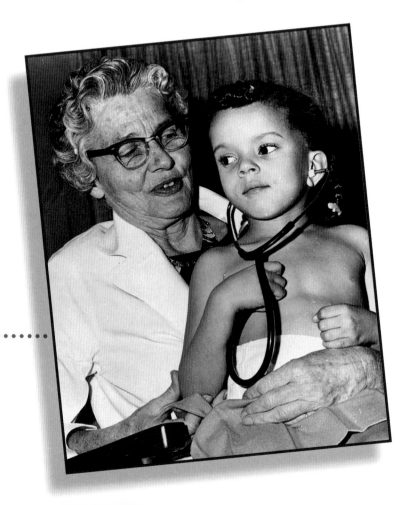

Helen was known as a very caring physician. She became deeply involved in the lives of her young patients and their families. She believed that a strong relationship between a doctor and her patient was an important part of the healing process.

Helen's responsibilities at the hospital included teaching doctors pediatric cardiology. After the success of the blue baby operations, doctors flocked to study under her. Each year, Helen supervised the training of several American and foreign doctors.

At age sixty-four, Helen took to the public stage in her efforts to protect children's health. She informed the American people about the dangers of the drug thalidomide. Committed to public service, Helen was a member of the World Health Organization and other health groups. In 1986, she was setting out to drive some senior citizens to vote when she was killed in a car accident.

BACKGROUNDER

Thalidomide

In 1962, one of Helen's former students working in Germany told her about the birth defects he was seeing in his practice. The cause was thought to be a drug given to pregnant women. Known in North America as thalidomide, the drug was not yet being sold in the United States. Helen decided to look into the situation herself. She traveled to Europe in 1962 and examined children born with deformed arms or legs. When she returned to the United States, she reported that thalidomide was probably causing these defects. Thalidomide was banned throughout the world in 1962.

"I personally feel, and I think I have proven, that if you can make your contribution and do significant work, the world will respect you, men and women alike."

More Women in Profile

The following pages list a few more women in medicine you may want to read about on your own. Use the Suggested Reading list to learn about these and other women in medicine.

1901–1963
Dorothy Anderson
American Pathologist

Working as a **pathologist** at Babies Hospital in New York, Dorothy began to notice children who had an abnormal pancreas, a large gland near the stomach. She discovered they were all suffering from an unknown disease, which Dorothy named cystic fibrosis. Dorothy developed a simple way to test children for cystic fibrosis. Doctors still use this test today.

1909–1974
Virginia Apgar
American Physician

In 1952, Virginia created the Apgar score, a test designed to **diagnose** any problems in babies immediately after birth. Doctors were to check for any heart, muscle, or breathing problems. Virginia used the letters of her last name for what was to be checked in each category: appearance, pulse, grimace, activity, and respiration. Doctors throughout the world now use the Apgar score to detect problems with infants as early as possible.

1873–1945
Sara Josephine Baker
American Physician and Public Health Pioneer

As a young **physician** in the early 1900s, Josephine worked as a medical inspector in the slums of New York City. She set up health stations, where babies received milk and medical exams. Her work saved thousands of infants who would otherwise have died. When the city created a child health unit, Josephine became its director. She was the first woman to hold a senior position in an American health department.

Dr. Virginia Apgar

1924–

Jewel Plummer Cobb

American Cell Biologist and Educator

Jewel has made important contributions in both medicine and education. She carried out cancer research that paved the way for later developments in **chemotherapy**. As an educator, she has worked to make it easier for minorities and women to get an education in the sciences. Jewel has written about how, for centuries, society has discouraged young girls from pursuing careers in math and science. An inspirational leader, Jewel served as president of California State University at Fullerton in the 1980s.

1895–1982

Anna Freud

Austrian Child Psychoanalyst

The youngest child of the famous **psychoanalyst** Sigmund Freud, Anna started her career as a teacher. She was also trained by her father in his ways of treating mental disorders. After her father died, Anna continued his work. She also made important contributions of her own. At her clinic in England, Anna helped children cope with loss and fear.

1956–

Mae Jemison

American Astronaut and Physician

Mae became the first African-American woman to fly in space. Before her training as an astronaut began in 1987, Mae worked as a **physician** in Los Angeles. Aboard the spacecraft *Endeavour* in 1992, Mae carried out experiments on the effect of weightlessness on animals such as frogs, fish, flies, and humans.

Mae Jemison

1880–1952

Elizabeth Kenny

Australian Nurse

Elizabeth worked with **polio** victims in Australia. She developed a new way of treating people whose arms and legs were paralyzed by polio. Instead of setting their limbs in casts or splints, she used moist heat and exercise therapy. At first, some doctors criticized her approach. Eventually, her method became widely accepted. Elizabeth opened clinics in her native Australia, then in England and the United States.

1944–

Antonia Novello

American Physician

In 1989, President George Bush nominated Antonia as surgeon general of the United States. She was the first woman to serve in this office. Born and raised in Puerto Rico, Antonia had done a lot of work with children infected with **AIDS**. As surgeon general, she drew attention to important health issues, such as the dangers of smoking and of teenagers using alcohol.

Dr. Antonia Novello

1871–1953

Florence Sabin

American Medical Researcher

Florence was one of the first women to graduate from Johns Hopkins Medical School in Maryland. While still a medical student, she created a model of the human brain that is still being used in medical schools throughout the world. A highly regarded researcher, she was the first woman to be appointed a full professor at Johns Hopkins. In her seventies, Florence started a new career in public health. She helped introduce health laws in Colorado that have served as a model for other states.

1918–

Cicely Saunders

British Physician and Founder of Hospice Movement

Cicely started her career as a nurse. She then worked as a medical social worker and finally became a **physician**. In the late 1940s, Cicely set out to improve the care of the dying. She decided to set up her own hospice, a place where dying people could be given loving care. The success of Cicely's hospice inspired people in Britain and North America. Now there are thousands of hospices in the world. In 1980, Cicely was given the honorary title "Dame of the British Empire" in recognition of her work.

1910–

Annie Dodge Wauneka

American Public Health Educator

A Navajo Native-American, Annie introduced modern medicine to her people in the 1940s and 1950s in the southwestern United States. Tuberculosis, a highly catching lung disease, was ravaging the Navajo community. Through education, Annie showed her people how to fight the disease. She pointed out the importance of clean food and water. A tribal councilor, Annie was the first Navajo woman elected to public office. In 1963, Annie received the Presidential Medal of Freedom for her leadership in health care.

1947–

Flossie Wong-Staal

Chinese Medical Researcher

Flossie is one of the top experts in the study of viruses. Born in China and raised in Hong Kong, she moved to the United States to study medicine. When the **AIDS epidemic** was recognized in the early 1980s, Flossie began researching the disease. She discovered the virus that causes AIDS. Currently, she is working on finding a vaccine for AIDS.

Flossie Wong-Staal

Glossary

AIDS: a disease which destroys the body's ability to fight disease and infection

anatomy: a science that studies the structure of animals and plants

artery: one of the vessels that carries blood away from the heart to all parts of the body

apprentice: a person who works for a skilled worker in order to learn a trade or skill

birth control: various methods for controlling the number of children a woman has

chemotherapy: the treatment or control of disease with chemicals

colony: a region ruled by a distant country

communist: a person with the belief that the state, rather than a few individuals, should control the means of production in a country

concentration camp: a camp where prisoners of war or enemies of the government are kept

diagnose: to find out what disease or ailment a person is suffering from

dissect: to cut up carefully in order to examine

epidemic: the very fast spread of a disease

intern: a doctor who has just graduated from medical school and is working in a hospital under more experienced doctors

leukemia: cancer of the blood cells

pathologist: a specialist who studies the causes and effects of disease

pediatric cardiology: the study of heart problems in children

phosphorus: a poisonous substance that glows faintly in the dark

physician: a doctor

physiology: the study of living things, their parts, and their functions

polio: a disease that affects the spinal cord

proteins: important molecules that have many functions and are found in all living cells

psychiatrist: a doctor who treats mental illness

psychoanalyst: a specialist who treats people with mental problems by encouraging them to talk about their feelings

smallpox: a disease causing a fever and blister-like spots on the skin

stethoscope: an instrument used for listening to the heart and lungs

Suggested Reading

Gill, Derek. *Quest: The Life of Elisabeth Kübler-Ross*. New York: Harper & Row, 1980.

Haber, Louis. *Women Pioneers of Science*. New York: Harcourt Brace Jovanovich, 1979.

Lindrop, Laurie. *Dynamic Modern Women: Scientists and Doctors*. New York: Twenty-First Century Books, 1997.

Marks, Geoffrey, and William K. Beatty. *Women in White: Their Role as Doctors through the Ages*. New York: Charles Scribner's Sons, 1972.

McGrayne, Sharon Bertsch. *Nobel Prize Women in Science*. New York: Birch Lane Press, 1993.

O'Hern, Elizabeth Moot. *Profiles of Women Scientists*. Washington, D.C.: Acropolis Books, 1985.

Spoerry, Anne. *They Call Me Mama Daktari*. Norval, Ont.: Moulin Publishing, 1996.

Stille, Darlene R. *Extraordinary Women of Medicine*. New York: Children's Press, 1997.

Stille, Darlene R. *Extraordinary Women Scientists*. Chicago: Children's Press, 1995.

Kramer, Rita. *Maria Montessori: A Biography*. New York: Addison-Wesley, 1988.

Index

1 2 3 4 5 6 7 8 9 0 Printed in Canada 8 7 6 5 4 3 2 1 0 9